Taylor Swift
Lisa Rose
childsworld.com

Published by The Child's World®
800-599-READ • www.childsworld.com

Copyright © 2026 by The Child's World®
All rights reserved. No part of this book may be reproduced or utilized in any form or by any means without written permission from the publisher.

Photography Credits
Photographs ©: Darryl Dyck/The Canadian Press/AP Images, cover, 1; Thomas Jackson/Alamy Live News/Alamy, 5; Shutterstock Images, 6, 8, 19, 20, 23, 27; Rick Diamond/ACMA2013/Getty Images for ACM/Getty Images Entertainment/Getty Images, 11; Christopher Polk/Getty Images for PCA/Getty Images Entertainment/Getty Images, 13; Brian Cantoni/Flickr, 14; Carla Sloke/Shutterstock Images, 17; Ian West/PA Wire/AP Images, 25; Theo Wargo/WireImage/Getty Images, 29; Design elements from Shutterstock Images

ISBN Information
9781503875692 (Reinforced Library Binding)
9781503876712 (Portable Document Format)
9781503877214 (Online Multi-user eBook)
9781503877832 (Electronic Publication)

LCCN 2025938201

Printed in the United States of America

ABOUT THE AUTHOR
Lisa Rose cannot sing like Taylor Swift. However, like Swift, she loves cats. She has two black cats that helped her write this book.

TABLE of CONTENTS

CHAPTER ONE

Swift's World . . . 4

CHAPTER TWO

Early Years . . . 10

CHAPTER THREE

***Fearless* Star . . . 16**

CHAPTER FOUR

Pop Sensation . . . 22

Glossary . . . 30

Fast Facts . . . 31

One Stride Further . . . 31

Find Out More . . . 32

Index . . . 32

CHAPTER ONE

Swift's World

Taylor Swift spent about 6 months preparing for the Eras Tour. It was her biggest concert tour yet. She built up strength at the gym. She ran on a treadmill while singing her songs aloud. She also took dance lessons. It was hard work singing and moving across a large stage at the same time. These activities would help her practice for the real thing. Finally, on March 17, 2023, it was time. Swift waited backstage at her show. She heard the roar of the crowd as she got into position. They were cheering her name. Swift was excited. She was ready to perform for fans across the world once again.

The Eras Tour started in Glendale, Arizona, and ended in Vancouver, Canada. The tour had 149 shows across five continents. It earned more than $2 billion.

Many fans dressed up in different styles for the Eras Tour. Some wore styles inspired by particular albums, such as *Lover* or *reputation.*

The Eras Tour was Swift's sixth concert tour. But this tour was different. It was a celebration of all her albums and the different styles of music she had created over the years. Each concert was 3.5 hours long and featured more than 40 songs. The songs were selected from each era of her career. In May 2024, Swift added songs from her latest album, *The Tortured Poets Department*.

Fans across the world loved the Eras Tour. They enjoyed the production, songs, and performances. The tour also brought visitors to cities and helped local businesses thrive. Many places set up Swift-themed events and sold items to fans going to concerts.

On the Eras Tour, fans traded Taylor Swift–themed friendship bracelets. Some fans even wrote Swift's lucky number, 13, on their hands.

Many of Swift's fans, called Swifties, were not able to attend an Eras Tour concert. But Swift found a way for them to join in the fun, too. A movie called *Taylor Swift: The Eras Tour* released in 2023. It brought the experience of the Eras Tour to the big screen. Swift filmed three performances in August 2023 at SoFi Stadium in California. The movie was about the length of an Eras Tour concert. When the film hit theaters on October 13, 2023, it quickly became a huge hit. The film earned $261.7 million worldwide.

The Eras Tour was a celebration of all Swift had accomplished so far in her career. The singer-songwriter started her career in country music. She later transitioned to pop. No matter the era, Swift has pushed through challenges, broken records, and won awards. Swift is a superstar who has made her mark on the music industry.

SWIFT'S CATS

Taylor Swift loves her pet cats. She says they help her relax. Swift got her first cat, Meredith Grey, in 2011. She got Olivia Benson in 2014. And she got Benjamin Button in 2019. All three cats are named after TV or movie characters. The cats have appeared in music videos and commercials with Swift.

CHAPTER TWO

Early Years

Taylor Swift was born on December 13, 1989, in West Reading, Pennsylvania. Taylor's parents are Scott and Andrea Swift. Scott worked as a stockbroker, and Andrea was a homemaker. Andrea later helped manage Taylor's career. Taylor also has a younger brother named Austin. From an early age, the Swift family supported Taylor's love for music and helped her follow her dreams.

When Taylor was little, she loved to sing Disney songs every chance she got. But when she heard Shania Twain's voice, Taylor fell in love with country music. She loved listening to Faith Hill, The Chicks, and LeAnn Rimes. Young Taylor watched their music videos and learned their songs, too.

Swift's parents have been her biggest supporters. Scott and Andrea attended the Academy of Country Music Awards in 2013 with Swift.

Taylor wanted to get serious about performing. Her parents took her to acting and singing lessons. She performed anywhere she could. This included local fairs, festivals, and sporting events. Taylor also did musical theater. She acted in school productions. She performed in shows with a group called the Berks Youth Theatre Academy. Some of the shows included *Grease*, *Annie*, and *The Sound of Music*.

CHRISTMAS TREE FARM

When Taylor Swift was a child, she lived on a Christmas tree farm. Taylor loved growing up on the farm and riding horses. Her parents and her younger brother all helped on the farm. This made her family very close. It was young Taylor's job to pick praying mantis eggs off Douglas fir trees. This was so they would not hatch inside people's homes and give them a buggy Christmas surprise!

Swift has a close relationship with her brother, Austin. In 2011, Austin attended the People's Choice Awards with Swift.

When Taylor was 11 years old, she convinced her parents to visit Nashville, Tennessee. Nashville is known as the capital of country music. Taylor had recorded demos. These are recordings that show a musician's work. She dropped her demos off at recording companies. She hoped one of them would offer her a **record deal**. But that did not happen.

In 2007, Taylor visited the headquarters of the internet company Yahoo in Sunnyvale, California, and played at a lunchtime concert.

Taylor did not give up, though. She realized she should stop trying to sound like other singers. She needed to develop her own style. Taylor learned how to play the guitar when she was 12 years old. She began writing her own songs. Taylor had always loved writing poems. She realized she could turn her poems into music. She also turned her diary entries into songs. Taylor bravely shared her feelings with the world through her music.

Taylor's hard work paid off. At 13, she was offered a development deal by RCA Records. A development deal is not the same as a record deal. A company agrees to keep an eye on an artist. After a year, the company decides whether to give the artist a record deal, tell them no, or wait longer to decide. The development deal was a big step for Taylor's career. But after a year, RCA was not willing to give Taylor a record deal. She decided to keep looking.

At 14 years old, Taylor signed a songwriting deal with Sony/ATV Publishing. She was their youngest ever staff writer. As a staff writer, Taylor would have the chance to work with other songwriters. She got to learn from them and improve her skills. In 2003, Taylor's family moved to Nashville. They wanted to support her dreams. Taylor's journey to superstardom had only just begun.

CHAPTER THREE

Fearless Star

Taylor's songwriting success was growing. But she did not want her company to sell her songs to other singers. She wanted to sing them herself. Things changed in 2004. Taylor performed at the Bluebird Café. Many country stars have been discovered at the famous Nashville music **venue**. Music **executive** Scott Borchetta was in the audience that night. He knew Taylor was something special. He was starting a new record label called Big Machine Records. He wanted Taylor to be its first star. She agreed. Taylor finally had a record deal! Taylor released her first **single**, "Tim McGraw," in 2006. She was only 16. Her first album, *Taylor Swift*, came out later that year.

Taylor has often returned to play at the Bluebird Café.

Taylor Swift's **debut** album broke records upon its release. She gained many young fans. They related to her songs. The album peaked at number five on the *Billboard* 200. The *Billboard* chart keeps a list of the top US music hits. Taylor also charted in several countries, including Australia, Canada, and the United Kingdom. During this time, Taylor went on tour to open for Rascal Flatts. She later opened for music stars Tim McGraw and Faith Hill, too.

In 2008, Taylor released her second album, *Fearless*. "You Belong With Me" and "Love Story" were two of the hit songs on the album. It became the most awarded country album of all time. In 2009, Taylor went on the *Fearless* Tour to bring her music to live audiences. She traveled across the United States. Many fans were excited to hear her perform.

In 2009, Swift performed at Madison Square Garden in New York on the *Fearless* Tour.

In 2010, Swift performed at the Entertainment Industry Foundation Women's Cancer Research Fund. At the event, she took pictures with Tim McGraw (center) and Faith Hill (right).

In 2010, Taylor attended the Grammy Awards. The Grammy Awards is music industry's biggest awards show. It was a very special night for Taylor. She performed with music star Stevie Nicks. Together, they sang "Rhiannon" by Fleetwood Mac and Taylor's hit song "You Belong With Me." *Fearless* won Taylor her first two Grammy Awards. Grammy Awards recognize a musician's achievements. Taylor won Album of the Year and Best Country Album. During Taylor's acceptance speech, she thanked her family who helped her along the way.

Taylor received more awards for *Fearless*. She won the Country Music Association Award for Album of the Year. She also won two Teen Choice Awards for Female Artist and Music Album of the Year. With all these achievements, things were looking up for the country star.

BEST FRIENDS FOREVER

Taylor Swift's best friend is Abigail Anderson Berard. They met on the first day of ninth grade. They sat next to each other in English class. They have been close friends since that day. Taylor wrote a song called "Fifteen" about their friendship, mentioning "a redhead named Abigail" in the lyrics. In July 2023, Abigail came to an Eras Tour performance. Taylor dedicated her performance of "Fifteen" to her longtime friend in the audience.

CHAPTER FOUR

Pop Sensation

Swift released the hit album *Red* in 2012. She was at the top of the country music world. But she wanted more. *Red* had included several songs with more of a pop sound. Swift decided to lean into this new sound. She wanted to make a pop album. Many fans and critics thought she was making a mistake. Some thought she might fail. But her next album, *1989*, became a top seller. It won Album of the Year at the Grammy Awards in 2016. Some hit songs from the album included "Shake It Off," "Bad Blood," and "Blank Space."

Swift attended the Grammy Awards in 2016. It was held at the Staples Center in Los Angeles, California.

Swift celebrated *1989*'s success. But in 2016, she was involved in a **scandal**. Back in 2009, Swift had won her first Video Music Award. Rapper Kanye West interrupted her acceptance speech. He said pop star Beyoncé should have won the award instead. West and Swift made up after the incident. But in 2016, West released a song with rude lyrics about Swift. The song said he was the one who made her famous. Swift publicly **criticized** him.

IN HER WORDS

In an interview with *CBS Sunday Morning*, Taylor Swift talked about how women are treated differently than men in the music industry. She said:

> **There's a different vocabulary for men and women in the music industry, right? A man does something, it's strategic. A woman does the same thing, it's calculated. A man is allowed to react. A woman can only overreact.**

Source: Donnelly, Erin. "Taylor Swift Calls Out Music Industry Sexism: 'A Man Is Allowed to React. A Woman Can Only Overreact.'" Yahoo Entertainment, *August 25, 2019. www.yahoo.com.*

Swift performed at Wembley Stadium in London, United Kingdom, on her *reputation* Stadium Tour in 2018.

But West's wife, Kim Kardashian, revealed another side of the story. She shared recordings of Swift talking to West about the song and giving her approval. Swift said she had not heard the whole song. But many people felt Swift had not been honest about what happened. Swift stepped out of the public eye afterward.

What the public did not know was Swift was pouring her feelings into new music. In 2017, Swift surprised everyone with her sixth album, *reputation*. It dropped with no warning. Swift did not do interviews about the album. But it was still a success. The album won a *Billboard* Music Award for Top Selling Album. It also won an American Music Award for Favorite Pop Album.

In 2018, Swift's record deal with Big Machine Records ended. She decided to join a different record label. Part of why she did this was to control her masters. Masters are the original recordings of songs or albums. Artists who own their masters have more control over their songs. They also earn more money when the songs are bought. Going forward, Swift would own the masters for her new music. But Big Machine still owned the masters for her first six albums.

In 2019, **music manager** Scooter Braun bought Big Machine. This meant he owned the recordings. Swift had clashed with Braun in the past. She thought he was a bully. She did not want him to earn money from her music. She decided to rerecord her own songs. She released her old albums as Taylor's Versions. Braun would still earn money off the old versions. But Swift hoped to push them out of use with the new versions. Swift released *Fearless (Taylor's Version)* and *Red (Taylor's Version)* in 2021. *Speak Now (Taylor's Version)* and *1989 (Taylor's Version)* came in 2023. These rereleases topped the charts. It showed how strong the staying power of Swift's music really was.

SWIFT'S ALBUMS

Taylor Swift has released many songs and albums throughout her music career. Some of her albums have won the Grammy Award for Album of the Year (AOTY):

2006
Taylor Swift

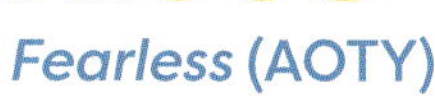

2008
Fearless (AOTY)

2010
Speak Now

2012
Red

2014
1989 (AOTY)

2017
reputation

2019
Lover

2020
folklore (AOTY)
evermore

2021
Fearless (Taylor's Version)
Red (Taylor's Version)

2022
Midnights (AOTY)

2023
Speak Now (Taylor's Version)
1989 (Taylor's Version)

2024
The Tortured Poets Department

In addition to rerecording her old music, Swift continued producing new music. She released *Lover* in 2019 and two more albums in 2020. In 2022, she released *Midnights*, which later won the Album of the Year at the Grammy Awards in 2024. Even performing on the Eras Tour did not stop Swift from creating new music. *The Tortured Poets Department* came out while Swift was on tour in 2024. And on May 31, 2025, Swift shared exciting news. She had officially purchased all of her old master recordings. For the first time in her career, all of Swift's music belonged to her.

A CAREER IN ACTING

Taylor Swift has had several acting roles. She made her acting debut in 2009 on the TV show *CSI: Crime Scene Investigation*, where she played a rebellious teenager. In 2010, she acted in the movie *Valentine's Day*, where she played a high school student. In 2012, Swift voiced a character named Audrey in the animated movie *The Lorax*. She also appeared in the 2019 movie musical *Cats*, where she played a character named Bombalurina. Swift's acting roles have helped her connect with fans in new and exciting ways.

Swift played Bombalurina in *Cats*. She sang a song called "Beautiful Ghosts."

Swift's career has had many eras. She has been a superstar in all of them. Her fans look forward to seeing what she will do next!

GLOSSARY

calculated (KAL-kyoo-lay-tuhd) Something calculated is well thought out or planned, and the word is usually used in a negative way. Swift said women in the music industry are called calculated but men are called strategic.

criticized (KRI-tuh-sized) Someone or something is criticized if it is examined and judged closely. Swift criticized Kanye West for his lyrics about her.

debut (day-BYOO) A debut is the first time someone performs or shows something to the public. Swift's debut album made her famous.

executive (ig-ZEK-yuh-tiv) An executive is a person who makes important decisions in a company. Swift worked with an executive to plan her new album.

music manager (MYOO-zik MAN-ij-er) A music manager is a person who helps a musician with their career and business. In 2019, music manager Scooter Braun bought Big Machine Records.

record deal (REH-kurd DEEL) A record deal is an agreement between a recording artist and label. Swift made a record deal with a company to release her music.

scandal (SKAN-dl) A scandal is something that causes people to be upset or shocked. Swift released *reputation* after her scandal with Kanye West.

single (SING-ul) A single in music is a song that is released separate from an album. Swift released her first single, "Tim McGraw," in 2006.

strategic (struh-TEE-juk) Something strategic is well thought out or planned, and the word is usually used in a positive way. Swift said men in the music industry are praised for being strategic.

venue (VEN-yoo) A venue is a place where events happen, such as concerts or games. Swift's concert at the venue was huge.

FAST FACTS

- Taylor Swift was born on December 13, 1989, in West Reading, Pennsylvania.
- When Taylor was 11 years old, she convinced her parents to take her to Nashville, Tennessee. She dropped demos off at recording companies. Taylor learned to play guitar at age 12 and began writing her own songs.
- Taylor's first album, *Taylor Swift*, came out in 2006. It had popular songs including "Tim McGraw." Taylor fully switched from country music to pop music with her album *1989*.
- After Scooter Braun bought her old record company, Swift re-recorded her first six albums as Taylor's Versions to gain more control over her music.
- The Eras Tour started in March 2023 and ended in December 2024. It had 149 shows across five continents. It became the highest-grossing tour ever, earning more than $2 billion.

ONE STRIDE FURTHER

- Think about times when Swift overcame challenges in her life. How did she push through them? Why was it important that she did not give up?
- Swift loves to write songs. Why do you think the songs Swift wrote were important to her? Why do you think Swift's songs connect with so many fans?
- Music is very important to Swift. What is something that is important to you? How can Swift's story inspire you to work hard for something you find important?

FIND OUT MORE

IN THE LIBRARY

Anderson, Kirsten. *Who Is Taylor Swift?* New York, NY: Penguin Random House, 2024.

Loggia, Wendy. *Taylor Swift.* New York, NY: Golden Books, 2023.

Nguyen, Suzane. *Taylor Swift.* Bloomington, MN: Bellwether, 2025.

ON THE WEB

Visit our website for links about Taylor Swift:

childsworld.com/links

Note to Parents, Caregivers, Teachers, and Librarians: We routinely verify our web links to make sure they are safe and active sites. So encourage your readers to check them out!

INDEX

awards, 9, 18, 20–21, 22, 24–25, 27, 28

Big Machine Records, 16, 26
Bluebird Café, 16
Borchetta, Scott, 16
Braun, Scooter, 26

Eras Tour, 4, 7–9, 21, 28

Fearless, 18, 20–21, 26, 27

Lover, 27, 28

Midnights, 27, 28

Nashville, Tennessee, 13, 15–16
1989, 22, 24, 26, 27

Red, 22, 26, 27
reputation, 25, 27

Swift, Andrea, 10
Swift, Austin, 10, 12

Taylor Swift, 16, 18, 27
Taylor's version, 26, 27
Tortured Poets Department, The, 7, 27, 28